ACCIDENTAL GARDEN

ACCIDENTAL GARDEN

POEMS

CATHERINE ESPOSITO PRESCOTT

GUNPOWDER PRESS • SANTA BARBARA
2023

Published by Gunpowder Press
David Starkey, Editor
PO Box 60035
Santa Barbara, CA 93160-0035

Cover image: Courtney Smith

ISBN-13: 978-1-957062-06-8

www.gunpowderpress.com

For Connor, Austen, and Celia

Contents

I.

Earth Day, 2020

In quarantine, we noted how the raccoons use
the garden hose at night and shift the nozzle

to their desired setting, which is shower,
a gentle, cleansing water, which is opposite to the jet

that cleans their scat off the backyard deck
under the fence of fishtail palms.

In quarantine, saw-toothed sharks—prehistoric
predators known for living in the depths of ocean

far from humans, swam close to shore
along with nurse sharks and bull sharks.

In quarantine, manatees surfaced in pairs,
dolphins leapt out of the water three, four

at a time without the promise of snacks in sight,
no prize, no bucket of fish, which tells us

something about reward, a thing given
for forced labor, and another about joy—

how it comes on its own, comes without us
begging for it—how it's more like a country, wide

and prosperous, than a summer fair. Our blind spots
are infinite. What we don't know is more cave than dot.

When was the last time I moved my body—for no camera,
no post—for nothing more than the rapture of being?

How do I know the raccoons don't find pleasure
in their hose shower? Why do I believe their paw prints

are evidence of trespass and escape,
not of skilled, choreographed feet—

every mud-print not a direction, not a clue,
but a turn toward ecstasy?

6 AM

Our electric car hums.
My boys drape their eyelids
over unfinished dreams.

The sun is a rumor. The sky blinks
with hunters, warriors, and every human's fate,
ancient mappings of this world,

which my boys would never accept
as truth unless it were proven in a TED Talk
or a self-appointed scholar's YouTube video.

My boys are a ram and a twin,
one thinks the other is his mate,
the other is stubborn and solitary.

I would tell them as much,
but they're not listening; their eyes
turn in and out of sleep.

As we approach the bus stop,
the car is stone-quiet. Before they walk
away, I want to say something

like *carpe diem* but wittier,
like *This moment is all we have*, but less alarmist,
like *Be both the lion and the lamb*.

I want to speak in metaphors
and aphorisms that will bloom in their minds
during third period, to singe them with grace.

This morning, I'm searching
for a phrase that's both spark and amulet,
but the silence between us

insists on staying empty
like a bowl of air carrying
the gentle charges of neutrons, electrons,

and protons, deeper quarks
and nucleons, the atomic and subatomic strata
pulsing inside layered atoms,

every energetic particle
moving in its own orbit,
maintaining an essential distance

from the others, so the entirety
doesn't collapse. These are distances
we have yet to measure—

the boys and I, and the world
outside, the invisible threads of all
I must leave unsaid.

Sea Turtles

Lifeguards erect flag fences around holes
the width and depth of a human head,
holes filled with piles of eggs you'd swear
look like buckets of ping-pong balls.

One night, when the full moon is high,
hatchlings will stumble to sea if guided
by moonlight, not fooled by manmade streetlights
or lights from an oceanfront condo.

They will survive for another generation,
live a slow-aging life not unlike ours.
Female sea turtles lay their eggs on the same beach
where they were born. Scientists don't know

how they find home. Is it the taste and feel of the water?
Temperature of the sand? Some other feeling as yet
undetectable to humans? Turtle pulse and hiss?
When all grown, I don't know if my children

will remember the beach where they were born,
if they'll hurry to escape it for greener grasses,
or if they'll paddle back or if it will even be here—
where their lives began in a sunlit space,

tempered by palm trees and aquamarine,
where sand marked their first steps, and the ocean's howls
met their first screams. One day, which may
have been many, they ran toward the sea

with their half-dollar-sized fists raised,
and plastic shovels pitched like tritons—
to announce their voyage off to its depths
as if in an act of reverse evolution—

from toes to webbed feet, from lungs to gills
or as if headlong into an unseeable future—
or as if into the adventure of a lifetime—
or into the adventure of the moment—

into the forever-long now—their eyes
fixed on the paths they'd carve
through water, through land, the ones
that call from the soul's wild knowing.

The Early Years

I am a careless tourist here,
walking on top of insects, and
carpets of microscopic creatures.

I am heavy and uncoordinated.
Every stomp of my sneaker
mutilates a universe of microbes,

every step disperses seeds
and energy. I don't know how
to balance this account. I don't know

how the world works, how I raised
three children without a map,
pre-smart phones, without a guidebook.

Like the manatee with her calves,
I called to them, and they called back.
How it was: I had no words when they

had no language; I had no hands before
they found theirs. We spent years
at the beach wandering the shoreline,

imprinting our feet into sand, and watching
the ocean lick them clean. We screamed
into waves as if divining primal songs.

The world was as we imagined it to be:
beach balls turned into planets, the sand
glittered with shards of stars.

The Autograph Tree

Native to tropical America,
the species was named by Carl Linneas
after the botanist Charles de l'Écluse. Clusia
trees and bushes have large, waxy, elliptical leaves,
whose latex and resin are known to seal wounds. Favorite green
fence for the houses in my neighborhood, some of the oldest are like travel
logs at the end of a hiking trail, each leaf carved with initials and hearts
and 4EVAS. On one, a wizard's lightning bolt, on another the outline
of a joint, a sailboat, an "I ♥ U" and "baby girl" on another.
In Key West, we etched table numbers into leaves
for my sister's wedding. Adequate monuments,
the trees note every passing—the bud of new
love, even the most quiet hope. In polka-
dots of shade and pockets of sunlight,
in storm swells and hurricane winds,
the trees hold space, their branches
pull each leaf close and hold tight
as only love can do.

Palm Sunday

Rome, 2018

We walk along the Circus Maximus,
the remains of a chariot racetrack.
The stands once marble, now grass, held tens
of thousands. Today, our children run
up the blank hills and around the track.
We move as one unit each in our own body.
My husband harnessed to his thoughts,
our daughter leaping into air, one son kicking
rocks from foot to foot, the other listening
to scratchy music from thumb-sized earbuds.
It is easy for us to leave each other. We practice
daily. Our procession across ancient stones
is unsanctified. Palms wave overhead, pine trees
stand stoic. Generals, priests, decorated men
walked these roads millennia before us,
their achievements etched in time-worn stones.
As usual, the women are missing, their stories
uninscribed, so I try to infer how they lived
from the everyday gods they worshiped,
gods summoned like spices to a feast:
a goddesses of childbirth, a god who looked after the grain,
a goddess who watched children, one who helped
bread rise, one who accompanied children
out of the house and oversaw their safe return.
When my children leave home, I know I'll call
upon the goddess of crossroads and magic,
maybe the god of luck, and certainly the goddess
who will accompany them on their travels.

The descending sun paints the sky to a fresco.
Our children chase and tag each other,
a game that must predate this racetrack
of marble-turned-ruins. Meeting at the oval's apogee,
breathless, they ask us what's for dinner.

Aubade, South Beach

The beach carries scattered remains of the night—
a bedsheet, a beach blanket etched in sand. The shore
quivers with discarded cigarette butts, ash
of weed, ash of tobacco, a soup of bottles—
mostly plastic, some glass—water, beer, champagne,
more than one condom—crumpled, disheveled,
used or not. I walk lifting each item as artifact,
I struggle to shelve judgment and my instinct
to churn each into myth. Orbs of sunlight reveal
chicken bones, fish skeletons, the chipped halfshell
of a mussel, one ghost crab leg. We combed
the beach one year, throwing larger refuse
into large trash bags, then sifting through sand
for hidden debris the way we knew how to as mothers—
grain by grain, as we'd parted our children's hair
many times that year lifting nits and eggs
from soft threads, from hair which had not yet
known gel and dye. That day my son found
a lucky seed from Cuba via Africa, one that holds
the evil eye at bay, all who would cause him harm,
and a rosary made of brown crystals, each bead intact,
with a Christ, sullen, surrendered, spinning.
The ocean washes up more than memory.
What is held by sand travels into the ocean's body
and returns not as waste, not as sacrament. I would
not let him throw them out. How could I?
He was too young to know faith,
he who had never needed to pray.

Ode

the flock of wild lime-green parrots
the clusia hedge with fat, waxy leaves
the butterfly bush and porterweed
the milkweed which seems frail but hosts dozens of cocoons
the moon which has now set
the sun as it charges over the beach, turning the world on as it rises
using "it" instead of "she"—giving the feminine a break
the pen that works, the fingers that hold it
the teenage boys who grow their minds at school
the daughter with unicorn dreams
the husband also rising
the quiet morning, then the raucous afternoon
the evening with its petty arguments
the soccer, the climbing, the gymnastics
the beautiful bodies of children
the athletes who challenge gravity, who move beyond the mind's limitations
the mind that tries to sit still
the body that yokes
the genders, the skin colors, the dances, the songs, the languages in which
      the same thoughts are set to new music
the engineers & programmers who abet the artists
the eyes—of course—even as print gets smaller
the senses—interpreting
the chance run-ins, the surprise diagnoses, truths spoken
the healers who radiate compassion
the seekers who find new pathways to understanding
the concept of infinity, which I cannot grasp—
the universe unaware of pushing outward
I imagine my mind without boundaries, my heart without boundaries
a wall becomes mirage, a line something to jump over

infinity on a macro scale and a micro scale
beyond quarks, beyond matter as particles as energy as imperceptible waves,
     what if this unfolds infinitely—
what if the cells travel inward forever
the heart and its cosmos, the brain and its cosmos, keeping your world steady
when you pick up the children from school, cook some spaghetti
the children orbiting you, you orbiting them
the spaces between you, full, collapsed
breathing in their wonder, you exhale yours.

II.

Ode

For the many walls of this house where I write this. For the roof that holds the rain from disturbing my loves as they sleep. For the roof that captures the light of the nearest stars. For my pantry, stocked with non-perishable, storm-ready food. For the plants that scrub the air we breathe—inhaling what would harm us, exhaling what heals. For the phone that compensates for my busy, middle-aged brain. For the computer that flickers with the light of many candles, works, writes, and searches the world outside these walls and just beyond the thrust of my voice. For the sun that lifts over the ocean every damn day, and for the ocean and its many colors, its mysteries, its teeming with life, and its trying. For the ocean who carries our carbon like a mother taking on way more than her share. To the mountains of my dreams and to the cities of my youth. To the music of many languages charging the air, electrifying it with feeling after thought. To the eyes that can still see clearly, to this mind that holds onto spools of logic, makes a cat's cradle of them, then finds a page to hold it all. To the page which asks for nothing, to the pen that gives and gives, and to the hand which says yes and no and sometimes even when needling with pain, even when cursed with doubt, and continues to travel over this pale sea.

Birth

The chant pulls rivers down
my face. I say MA, I sing mother.
I am that; I am not that.
Time escapes. Photographs
turn in a flip book, fanning memory:
What happened to the baby?
His man hands reach for mine,
fingers once no larger than a rosemary needle.
This plant of mine/not mine
calls to me in the deepest voice,
voice of river rocks. I am
soul struck. When did he arrive?
Did I hold open the door?
No, I was the door.
I was the door.

Amnesty

Hard rain batters the landscape. Palm tree fronds droop like wigs of feathered hair. The ficus hedge heaves as its drunk leaves spit excess water. Puddles kiss the chassis of my car as we break water, parting tiny sea after tiny sea. My kids shiver in the back seat, wet and cold— and because I am their mother, I give them my dry shirt, my dry pants, and I drive home in my underwear, exposing the sickle of the scar at the base of my throat and the pout of my middle-aged belly. Right now, hundreds of mothers are crossing rain-swallowed roads to reach invisible borders with their children, offering small sips of water, their dry socks, their dry shirts. And then what? How do we comfort when there's nothing left to give? The maw of my country closes on them, severing child from mother. Stopped at a red light, I lean my head on the steering wheel and find a way to pray.

Currency

The guru says observe silence
to unfold the divine

peace of the mind. Ancient load bearers,
women perch coiled in rope, coiled in metal,

coiled in dress, women with words piled
in their throats, words stopped from flying out

by coins placed like wafers in their mouths—
women's words no longer for curing,

for cursing. This is how a woman saves
her currency, alters sacrament. They sit, eyelids folded,

gaze internal. I picture unspoken words
charging their bodies like the light of stars.

Inside, each churns, each travels
into the planetarium of the stilled

mind. The mind, the guru says, is a map
of the universe. The women sit

holding their silence tall,
their unspoken, a universe.

The Poem Sets an Intention

to remember the scent of the rocking chair
      where my grandmother drank her last Manhattan
on the porch filled with the honeyed light of dusk;

cabins stocked with inherited dishes and pots,
      thread-worn sheets, quilts sewn by great aunts
we never met—the one who made peach pie,

and demanded perfect etiquette
      from her nieces, her Georgia home,
an unauthorized finishing school for the girls

from Queens, and the one who was a little off,
      who only spoke with children,
who was confused and kind;

the lake whirling with rainbows of gasoline, smell
      of duck feathers, innovation, and decay,
wet wooden water skis, cousins sick with fear;

cards stitched with knicks and fingerprints,
      the sound of shuffling, the deck rising
into a bridge, then collapsing;

my mother's gin-and-tonic voice
      calling us to dinner, charred meat and
sulfuric, iceberg salad on the table,

next to bottles of French and Italian dressing,
      the sides sticky from the night before;
my grandfather ringing the firehouse bell,

drawing his grandchildren into a tug of war,
        mud turning our soles slick, lips bitten,
hair wet with lake water and sweat,

the winner was king; physical strength was
        a man's game, and tomorrow's
favorite was always an older boy cousin;

one summer I learned how to make
        raspberry jam in my grandmother's
kitchen. She boiled bushels of wild berries

down to a juice that was viscous and syrupy sweet.
        Bright magenta, molten like the core
of the Earth itself, if Earth were a woman;

when the first spoonful burned my lips,
        I took in the jam as I was taught,
my tongue cursing it all the way down.

After a Sunday Morning Rainshower

a harem
of peahens
digs in our
front yard
quiet as children
in church.
Pecking
through
perennial peanut
for insects,
darting eyes
to the perimeter
& back.
The peacock
yells &
carries on
a few
blocks
down,
his feathers
bulging
like an
athlete's pecs.
The peahens
seem to sigh.
When they shake
their heads,
their feathered,
fan-like crests
arch upward
like many mystified
eyebrows.

A Superhero's Origin Story

begins with a head injury, venomous snake
bite, a genetic mutation, or a dose
of radiation. Our hero, a bit dumbstruck,
tries to carry on as if nothing happened

because that's what humans do. We continue
because the brain is last to catch up to what
the body knows, to what the mind in every
cell screams up the chain. Truth is harder

to deny if you start to see telescopically,
or if you develop telepathy. An outsized ability,
like an arm doubling in length is impossible
to hide, which is why we love stories that make

knowing undeniable. Good rests in one body,
evil in another. Powers reveal themselves. Heroes
vanquish villains, all roles are clear. One body
isn't bifurcated, doesn't turn on itself

becoming a mystery for doctors to solve:
find the cancer in the blood, breast, etc., use
X, Y, Z to excise it, and A+D or maybe M
to treat it. And J medicine for life. The body

doesn't become chessboard and minefield,
only microscope and telescope, instruments
for probing and saving, not one life but many—
and the transformations when they occur

are overt—never like the inside of a mind
bursting with light at dawn, never a heart
expanding beyond its cage, never
a voice box opening to pour its story.

Stories

A cicatrix of scar tissue, a necklace of missing lymph nodes,
bare back of a mad woman chanting by the river's edge,
catwalking between dunes along a hem of shoreline,
divested of office clothes, gone the pencil skirt and
elegant silk blouse. Equally lost is the desire for tight
fabric, all synthetics—even sweat-wicking yoga pants,
guess-which-polymer bras—nothing that closes in, that
hugs my breasts, nothing with the word "wonder"
inscribed on the tag, nor with complicated instructions.
Jersey shirts, dresses, and tees or no clothes at all.
Knowledge arrives like seeds across the ocean. More luck
lands at my feet every year, or it dies. A woman is an ocean, a
mother before eggs are harvested, harboring sacs,
nesting thousands, which could become her mini-mes,
ova as portraits. We carry generations tucked inside the deep
prairie of our bodies—great-grandmother's habit of
queefing during sex, her passion for homemade ravioli, her
reflexes—the knee that pulsed when sitting, eyes that
sang when speaking failed, when the language she adopted
tripped off her tongue. The stories are too many, too
unsung, too untold for the telling is hard, the telling is beyond our
vernacular, folded into an untapped, microscopic chorus. In the
womb that begins before the womb, women sustain
xeroxed generations, which become beings who work, who
yearn for freedom, for meaning, to end the cycle, the
zig-zag that keeps us coming back to life—or not at all.

III.

Ode

Walt Whitman sang of the body. Let me sing of mine.
A structure... it's hard for a woman to speak of her body.

A wall, a fortress, a thing that exists, the main part
where attention drifts, perceptible—a figure, a body.

Is it more than the sum of its parts, more than organs,
muscle, sinew, skin, and bones? What makes a body?

A pelican rushed into the ocean, by which I mean crashed
into water, a feathered ball, a bomb, to take a fish body.

As a child in church, I walked with cupped palms, face lowered
down the church's aisle, its spine, to receive and ingest Christ's body.

When my children were newborns, we slept skin to skin,
my torso, a generous hammock for their jaundiced bodies.

Also, the unit of measurement women are held against, reduced to.
Fact: Most women I know have never felt at home in their bodies.

What lasts: My body of work.
What doesn't: My corporeal body.

Ancient seers saw many bodies in everyone, each a sheath,
each a covering, each a barrier between the body and its soul.

How I knew I'd write poems, how I knew the boy I had just met
would become my husband—all through the subtle logic of the body.

When stricken, when struck. When suppressed by a viral load,
when rife with a cancer, we say it failed. We blame the body.

Denied its planetary status, did Pluto become less than celestial,
less than an orbiting, spinning, luminous body?

O, shape-shifter. O, life-giver. O, lungs. O, heart.
There are not enough words, not enough stars to illuminate this body.

Luck and Unluck

When we found a hundred-dollar bill on the parking garage floor. When we searched the carambola tree for ripe fruit and found three. When the oncologist said the silent cancer was found, that it was treatable. When the farmer, in the Zen story, loses his horse the villagers say he's unlucky. When the farmer's horse returns the next morning bringing three wild horses with him, the villagers say he is lucky. When the farmer's son is thrown from one of the wild horses and breaks his leg, the villagers decide the man is unlucky. When a war breaks out, all the young men are conscripted to fight for their country, save the man's son, the one with the broken leg. Again, the man is lucky. Through years of luck and un-luck, the man's response to the villagers is never yes and never no. He nods and says maybe. I picture him doling out polite nods to the villagers—his friends and his neighbors—even to his family—each nod an acceptance, an offering to an unappeasable god.

Suprasternal Notch

an indentation
small concave
a bowl for air
to gather
to hide
to protect
the gland known
for its butterfly
shape rather
than its purpose
(to regulate
hormones and
metabolic functions)

mine is gone
occupied
by cancer cells
it was removed
from my body
this skin,
a raised line
as if raked through soil
a do not enter sign
interdit, forbidden
my notch
my saucer
guards
like one
of the furies
watching over
the part
of my body
that pre-
deceased it.

Scar

A jagged em-dash
in the center
of my collarbone

The pause
between actions

The curtain
between the known
and the unknown

A two-inch-long
raised ridge
balance beam
pursed lips

what remains
of the seam

where instruments
entered

cut malignant growths
and left the sleep-
induced cave
of my body

+

I am animal with appetite
and for cancer

I was kill—
meat and meaning

+

You are healthy,
the oncologist said,
you just got cancer

like unlucky dice
the wrong number
on a roulette wheel

+

I try to release the mind
to lease the mind
to ease the mind

to move
from reason to feeling
to being
to the out-breath, the in-breath

The cancer is not me
My thoughts are not me

+

And yet, a choir
inside of me—
every viable cell—

sang thank you
when the nodules
were found

thank you
as the needle pierced skin
to the needle
which sought truth
(a substance
viscous stubborn yellowed
like stale gold
murmuring a subterranean
plot to overtake
my body)

thank you
to the excision
to the surgeons
the nurses
the anesthesiologists
to the drugs
thank you
to my little death
in OR5
to waking up again
thank you
to the nausea
even to the pain
especially the pain

Follow-Up Visits

There are many ways to look
inside a body.
I've been scanned and opened.
Today, bloodwork
is how we enter.
Drawn every six months,
the numbers
deciphered, signs
of disease decoded,
we search for disappearance.
Each cell holds a half-shut door
where cancer fled.
We look for its shadow-prints,
its silhouettes, its bad-boy fedora-clad,
sinister-smiled, skinny-cigarette-smoking cells.
We look for the still-burning fire and the smoldering ashes.
I am told to believe I am healthy,
cured,
clean
because the mind
makes us, makes me, makes my cells
dance in ecstasy or betray my body,
so when I sing
I am the woman with medicine in her voice,
a voice that rains light, light that scours my body
until each organ shines,
no faithless trace—
and my body is an emptied mind,
a light-filled sky,
where there's nothing to mind, nothing the matter.

Instructions: How to Heal

Dismiss the pretense that you
brought this on yourself, that you
summoned this from the depths
of suffering. Disavow the notion

that you caused your disease. Disown
interpretation and explanations. Disentangle
fact from facile thinking, please. In fact,
feel free to disturb your world

with a philosophy of randomness.
The universe began because it was God's way,
the Big Bang, or a collusion of certain
wandering particles? You decide.

Disclaim stories that tell you that you lost
yourself. You were thriving, you were expressive,
you ate healthy foods, you were healthy, you are
healthy, you meditated, you were kind

to plants and animals and people,
you loved and you are love. Dispossess
old thoughts. Disagree openly. Disembark
into a new life. Disappear like a comet

if you must, but set no intentions. See clearly.
Disown disease; it is not you. Your thoughts
are not you. The scar on your lip/arm/leg/lung/throat
is not you. Disidentify. You are whole.

The Day I Lost My Fear of Death,

I made breakfast, coffee and toast.
I packed the kids' lunches and sent them off to school.
I practiced yoga, I wrote a few words.

I know I paid the electric bill.
I most likely argued with my husband.
I tripped over a soccer ball in the hallway.

Migrating birds trilled in our garden.
And we didn't know the extent
of the cancer living inside of me.

How can I say this? I felt that the world
could continue without me. The world
at large. The world of my home.

I saw how I could leave the life I made.
I saw the magic trick, the disappearing act.
I saw the veil, and it lifting ever upward,

how eyes could open to find
my physical presence or absence.
I can't tell you how many hours I played

peek-a-boo with my babies. How many times
we curtained our eyes. How we pressed the edges
of our palms together and released

them like doors flown open,
and the look of relief and joy and surprise we felt
at the sight of each others' body.

On the day I lost my fear of death,
I saw a rope connecting all beings,
I saw love in the fibers of the rope,

and I knew my children would survive.
I knew it the way you smell rain before it falls.
I knew it the way I sensed I was pregnant before skipping a period.

I knew for sure my life would end.
And then I cried—not for my life,
not for those who would miss me,

but because I'd failed to see it
even after writing so many poems,
even after hours seated in meditation:

the subject of every sonnet,
the mystery that keeps the stars apart,
the weight of the world and its engine.

Put it this way: think of the birth
of the universe, think of how that first light
still reaches us from billions of years away.

It enters us when we're putting away groceries,
taking out the trash, coaxing our loved ones to sleep.
It hit me while I was sorting laundry,

spreading clean sheets on the beds,
folding towels, and indulging in list making,
a stubborn form of hope, each word a tattooed promise.

The day I lost my fear of death, I knew
that this rope would carry me on,
would carry my people on. I would be

here and not here. I'd move from in front
of the curtain to behind it. From doer of all things,
I'd become memory, become daydream, become starshine.

IV.

Ode

after Wisława Szymborska

I prefer books.
I prefer children.
I prefer nonlinear to linear time.
I prefer waking up before sunrise.
I prefer cooking to take out.
I prefer handwritten notes to emails.
I prefer quiet punctuated by acoustic guitar strings or an aria.
I prefer the slow crescendo of a symphony.
I prefer love in every form.
I prefer to sit next to my daughter and smell the sun and sweat in her hair.
I prefer to watch my firstborn son come out of his funk and smile.
I prefer to see the world through my second son's eyes.
I prefer Sunday afternoons with my husband, the newspaper, and the
    crossword puzzle.
I prefer the excitement of travel to the comfort of my velvet couch.
I prefer listening to stories rather than telling them.
I prefer a night sky suffused with stars, planets, and soaring meteors.
I prefer to live in cities. (This is a contradiction.)
I prefer multiplication to division.
I prefer walking on the boardwalk to meditate on ocean waves spilling
    onto shore.
I prefer both the beach and the mountains. (I prefer not to choose.)
I prefer gardens inside my home and outside my home, plants and green
    everywhere I look.
I prefer oxygen. (This should go without saying.)
I prefer telling the truth—sometimes in pieces, sometimes whole.
I prefer staying silent when I don't know the answer.
I prefer dedicating time to my life's work, despite its foolishness.

I prefer to stretch with yoga and to run on the treadmill—sweating, releasing.

I prefer trust over distrust—even though it's not sensible nor very adult of me.

I prefer dessert after a meal with friends and family and a cappuccino or a
glass of port, if I'm truly happy.

I prefer to be here on this earth and in this poem with you than anywhere else.

I prefer to believe in possibilities beyond my observations.

Shark Valley

New Year's Day, 2018

Horizontal pock-marked rocks lie
in the shallow swamp like tombstones
to fallen alligators—as if to say Cassius
lived here, Orion slept there, and Sirius
ate turtles just beyond this path. We set
rocks to mark the long list of our dead.
Baby cocoplum leaves glow like strings
of holiday lights, each bush a lamp
in the growing darkness. As we bike
the 15-mile loop, headwinds push
the sun down the horizon, and the wind
whistles like an undaunted referee.
Last year, my brother-in-law did not die
of his cancer, and I did not die of mine.
The unrelenting wind presses against
our chests as if to warn us of the year ahead,
of what struggle, what pain, what loss
we will find buried in its days. For us,
the ones who have tasted the surgeons' knives,
there is no fear. We know how to leave
our bodies and how to return. Our bike
lights blink on and off, silent sirens
announcing our presence. No-see-ums
and mosquitos swarm. The wind slows
us, but we race forward as alligators slide
into the swamp and the last of the great egrets
flies to her dinner—her beak poised like a dagger,
every feather on her elegant body set to hunt.

Earrings

Three hoops twirl
like a mini galaxy
orbiting an unseen
star, orbiting each other,
their distances determined
by an artist's hands,
hands that strung seeds
from an acacia tree,
dried and dyed shades
of brown, hands
that curved metal
into circles like ellipses,
hands that took
what was given
and transformed it,
that dared to find another
expression for things
already wrought with beauty—
the star-shine metal,
the seeds charged
with genetic codes,
with the energy to grow
a thousand lives,
forests of trees,
every cell a library,
every cell a map of what could be
with the right amalgam
of water, soil, light.
My oldest son leaves
for college this fall.

A woman in India
makes copies
of the earrings
using seeds
from her garden.
She creates
jewelry from fallen
butterfly wings,
from seeds and leaves,
from what she finds
in the shadow of her guru.
She knows something of truth and beauty.
Her work is almost as difficult
to come by as a poem,
as impossible to recreate
as a seed becoming a certain tree,
an egg into that human,
minutes into one lifetime.

Reading To My Daughter About
Rocks and Gemstones Before Bedtime

Her fingers press into a photo of sandstone—
terra cotta-striped mountains, sculpted vases.

She forces her fists together to mimic how sedimentary
rock become metamorphic, how pressure turns limestone

into marble. We learn that obsidian is smooth, pumice floats,
and some geodes sparkle like the flesh of a ripe peach.

We travel underground to find rock deposits
clinging to earth like clumps of melted ice pops,

or dull jewels from discarded Elizabethan-era necklaces.
We learn that a diamond is concentrated carbon

cooked in the earth's mantle for at least one billion years.
Once mined, determined jewelers mar its surface

with hundreds of tiny cuts to make it sparkle.
She's old enough to know gemstones have greater currency

than rocks, and looks to me for confirmation.
Which do you like, Mama? The world will ask her

to choose over and over again. Even at my age,
I'm asked daily about Botox and hair dye.

In our city, there are more emergency, anti-aging
clinics than urgent care centers. She rests on the perch of my lap—

her first lookout. I cannot make these decisions for her.
I comb through her sun-streaked strawberry hair,

and try to answer every question eddying in the pools of her eyes—
You didn't answer, she yawns. She wants firm answers, a world of absolutes.

Do you know who made the rocks?, she announces, *God*.
Do we believe in God?, she says, turning the *v* into a *b*.

I was raised in a religion with many answers.
I was raised with self-abnegation, body as vessel,

body as original sin, a body made for birthing, for serving,
otherwise a thing to be distrusted, discarded.

Women were good or evil—and good was unattainable
for all but the saints, which meant the rest of us

were not good, or unworthy or undeserving,
which could also mean incomplete. I do not want

this for my daughter. When first born, babies see
black and white. Weeks later, colors separate—first ruby red,

last sapphire blue—but duality begins at birth. *We believe
in possibility*, I tell her. *We believe we don't know.*

I ride the line between honesty and security. I close
the book and watch her eyelids flutter to sleep, witness

her mind travel to dreamscapes where time
and gravity have no hold, the light insider her

a dynamic prism, a form beyond any earth-
bound formation, thinning the veil between us.

The Tattoos I'll Never Get

are legion: for my birth,
sleeves of mythological beasts,
muscled gods and goddesses
emerging from the sea,
an island for the sirens, a butterfly
for when I was becoming
and for the cancer removed,
for the sick gland, also removed,
ying and yang from the year I left
my religion, the names of old boyfriends,
of my dead, and my babies
written in wedding-invitation script across my forearms,
infinity symbols, a bracelet of laid-back
eights around my wrist,
one for each child and one for their dad.
I'm missing hearts, arrows, and stars.
I'm missing a Celtic
symbol for perseverance
and a Sanskrit word
to remind me of who I really am,
the self beyond groceries
and credit card payments,
self of the empty mind.
This morning I saw a rainbow backbend
over the earth's shoulder.
I would like to have this rainbow
etched across my back,
blade to blade. It would look over
the sun inked above
my tailbone, spiraled,

whirling, and ancient. I imagine
my tattoos awake, animated,
winking and whispering on the tapestry
of my body, a visual diary
of a life well lived or lived
like many others—part real, part
fantasy, all of it mine.

Accidental Garden

Did we plant a butterfly garden or did monarchs stumble on
the heirloom tomatoes that need pollen to transfer from pistil to stamen?
Big job, poor job to pollinate plants, without anthem, without a
bang, without music, an inaudible buzz. Flippant-seeming flutterers
have made this garden more than a green riot. I don't know an insect's
intention, but today we have bulbs of chocolate striped tomatoes, fistfuls
        of cherry
or grape tomatoes. I cannot remember which we planted; the forgotten
are numerous, are prolific, names of species, of genera. Sages say that
we all have consciousness—me, as the one who writes this—but also
a butterfly, a green parrot, an ant, a bee, our cat, and every tomato plant.
        Who is
divine? All of us scattered together on this earth like thrown dice—all
accident, all planned—with little more to do than to touch one thing,
        transform another.

The World

In the doctored video, a lion carries a baby monkey
to safety; though false, I want to believe in that world.

The organ is one thing, feeling another. The poet
says the latter must come first, his logic is so first world.

What if the seat of the mind resides here? What if thought
begins as feeling, wide enough to hold the world?

Once I felt light pour though my body; it gathered like a flash
mob at my sternum, a brilliant orb, then dissipated into the world.

I can love you and you and you and him and her.
You say love is a sense, a knowing, a complete world.

What is it Rumi wrote about the heart?
Yes, everything—his words, a world.

Picture the cakra a dot, then a bullseye widening to an arena
a city, a country, a continent, then the entire world.

When asked, "How should I treat others?," the saint
replied, "There are no others." I sit to know this world.

What is it? A door, a portal? All I know is that when it opens,
I startle toward you like a cat, then become the world.

New World Order

This time I'm trying
to not attach myself
to anyone or anything

I say *The table is not real*,
I say *The tree isn't real*,
the sky, too, even my

love isn't real—and there's
the problem with me. It's
coded in *my*. What a word—

as if I could ever own
anyone or anything,
as if my hands could hold

the world, feel its pulse,
and know it to be true.

Instructions: How to Give Things Away

Let's not get complicated about this. Let's not play
sentimental. The cracked toy car goes in the bag—
and seven more. Un-adored stuffed animals. Unworn t-shirts,
ones found in the crevice between the back of the dresser

and the wall. Any forgotten-thing automatically goes. The too-small
baseball bat, the trading cards, the deck of cards with a missing Jack,
unused roller blades, the CDs and VHS tapes we no longer play,
even books—the read-over-and-over ones, the broken-spine ones,

the frayed-pages ones. It's not easy shaking off the world. Soon, we'll have
nothing to hold us in place, no things to arm us, to define us,
to distract us. As our bags grow fat with first-world offerings,
we'll have less and less to take up space between us. We'll search

for only out-of-reach things, like the sun rising, the ocean as it combs
through your fingers, your voice climbing into and cupping, tenderly, my ear.

V.

A Word with God

I do not know much about Gods
but I want to find them:

the God in my coffee, the God in my tea,
the God in my children,

the God in my higher mind,
the God in my lower mind,

the God in my legs and arms,
the God in my fingers and toes,

in the parts of me that touch,
and that desire touch,

the God in my kitchen, God of electricity,
God of gas and fire, not brimstone,

the God of blasphemy, the God of truth,
of art, of poems, of the heart. Dear God,

please tell me about the organ
ballooning with breath. Is it mine?

Was I set sail with another's? Whose?
Whose body bristles with light?

I am open, dear God, whose light pours into me,
whose words? I am a sun, God.

part of a larger sun, a spoke in the wheel,
a thread in the fabric of being.

In this life, I've manifested wonder,
pinned words to the page,

made quilts of colorful sensations,
but none of these are me, are they?

I am a vessel. I've birthed so many.
Dear God, I am tired, I am eternal,

but I have work to do. What is work?
What is this poem but a tiny god?

And what is love, God, what is love?
May we have a word beyond words

now that my pen is out of ink, my mind un-
focused, and my heart, my heart,

like smoke at the end of a lit match?

Forgive Me,

I have coveted what's not mine. In dreams
I slipped my lips into cocoons of other lips
I entered another's mind
like a foreign country.

I know, these things don't happen
to people like us. We laugh, we cook,
we make love, we birth, we dance,
we get sick, we heal.

Love, my pores are ripening.
I am a sail with knife slits;
I am pierced at strange angles;
I don't know what this means.

I think this poem is a child, a toddler
stumbling like our children toward
a sliding-glass door. Remember the time
our son ran across head-first into the glass,

which looked like an open window?
Did you clean it? Did I? The illusion
of clear sky was so palpable, he believed
he would enter the outside

with no transition, by which I mean
he wouldn't have to open the door.
Is it closed now? It is open?
My mind is my least faithful organ.

This poem is the door. My face presses
into the glass; in my breath, these words
appear like fog lifting around the bay.
They are not what's underneath;

they are the fog, and I ride them as they lift.
(This is a false moment of clarity.)
This poem is not the child,
nor the door, nor the words breathed

into it. It exists insomuch as we
exist. We are more than witnesses
to our own dissolution. My mind navigates
a strange sea, and my flares are empty.

7 PM

at the Climbing Gym

He lifts one hand
to a peg
one foot to another
At the top of the wall
a silver bell
winks in florescence
as he swings
slips floats
from the wall
back and forth
like an idio-
syncratic
pendulum.
What matters
is not
that he arrives
at the top
but that he moves
toward it
when gravity
when will
pushes
pulls him
downward
With each
breath he
launches
forward

closer
to the summit
If I squint
he becomes
an astronaut
climbing
from star
to star
reaching for
every heaven

Black Creek Trail, or Annual Bike Ride During the Pandemic When Our Usual Route Is Closed

New Year's Day, 2021

Every vulture in Miami
congregates on the outskirts
of this landfill, and we ride
past their murder without speaking,
no, that is of crows, past their *wake*,
a *wake* of vultures, a *wake* which seems perfect
rather than prophetic—cloaked in
full black, full mourning regalia,
keeping vigil for this year—
or *wake* as in the thoughts
that simmer and spring me
into day before first light
or *wake* as in the Old English
wacu, the strong feminine,
to wake, to see.

Iguanas sit like sages
along the banks
of the polluted creek
which hugs the bike trail,
grown wiser from the ingestion
of toxins. This is the world
my boys will inherit, my boys,
almost full grown.
The trail takes a voyeur's
path through neighborhood
backyards with smoking BBQ pits,

loudspeakers singing salsa,
stacked plastic lawn chairs.

We pass perimeters of horse farms,
palm-tree farms, avocado farms
where egg-sized seeds turn
into towering trees.
We cross under highways,
over four-lane roads.
A homeless man tells my boys
love your mother first.
We bike through an encampment,
bus stops, condominiums,
a bird habitat designed with signs
adjacent to the creek
glittering with plastic bags.
A lone alligator appears and fades.
We have seen too much of each other.

At the end of the trail, we see
low-lying brush, no plant or tree
above eye level, yet thick with green.
The air is sweet, laced with baby's breath,
scent of the untouched, of beginnings.

My boys check their phones and laugh
when I sigh, mocking me with their gravel-voices,
their five-o-clock shadows, their minds
planning the ride back to our car,
and their years beyond our home, all
within arms reach. What seemed distant
is here. We didn't expect this view at the end—

not a clearing, not an emptiness,
no revelation to hold onto,
just resounding evidence
of seeds dropped into soil over and over.
We turn our bikes at the park's boarded-up
welcome center and ride out.

Sunlight falls from the sky, pitches
toward tomorrow. The boys
speed ahead, then wait for me
at the first street crossing
not because they must,
but to make sure I am safe.

I ride in the current of their wake.

Ordinary Offering

It's the most beautiful thing we do, she said
which meant carrying a spirit within our bodies,
which could also mean being possessed
by another. When pregnant with my daughter,

I craved chocolate and sex; with one son it was salted
meats and conversation, with the other son, milkshakes
and classical music. Each time their spirit left me
like a fierce wind, blowing the sail of my body

inside and out. For weeks after each birth, I rubbed
my empty torso like an unemployed crystal ball
whose answers were spent. Since then, scientists
have found a newborn's cells inside her mother,

and a mother's cells inside her baby.
Their fear is still my fear, their heartache and their joy, mine too.
I used to see quickening toddlers on leashes, one parent
steering the curious humans away from the street.

Every spring the wild peacocks tote a string
of newborn chicks behind them. Furry and dazed,
they follow their mothers like soldiers across
the cut-through street, from meal to meal.

Adolescent, they look like every other peacock,
their initial wobble grown to a tall strut.
Their full-feathered fans open into a many-eyed
sculpture, an ordinary offering to any god.

The Summer Before My Son Leaves for College

Rocky Mountain National Park, Estes Park, Colorado

I come from a sea-level civilization
and live in tune with the ocean's rhythms;
for hundreds of years my people
never sought higher ground, but today
my son and I step over rocks, finger
their formations to balance, to propel
our bodies further up the mountain
to Emerald Lake, a body of water bordered
by a mountain range and a waterfall
as tall as any building in the small
city where we live. At home,
the altimeter reads 1 ft. by our front door,
7 ft. from a friend's balcony, and -20, somehow,
on I-95. On this trail, we start our climb at 5,000 ft.
Our minds grow still as the climb grows steep.
Oxygen-thinned, we stop to take an extra breath,
to contemplate the chipmunk squatting on a rock,
to honor one dramatic mountain pass after another.
Words run dry—each time we pass a vista,
we shake our heads; it's too much,
the grandeur, the height of the mountains,
even our exertion, our reaching.
As air attenuates, thoughts part, company parts.
With every step, I feel us setting down
the things we carried for each other
for 18 years like stones.
Who was the son I thought I could raise?
Who was the mother he hoped I would be?

The sky turns light as we take in our final view—
a lake of clear water circled by jagged, snow-dotted peaks,
rivers of sunlight breaking through cloud cover,
a sheath of water cascading over the mountainside
feeding the lake—a landscape shaped by gravity
and time. At 10,000 ft, we begin to descend,
to lower our bodies toward the ocean.
I have done all I could. He is almost free.

Home

When I fell over the honeycomb
believing I entered a gold mine.

When I crossed the street tracing
the fossilized map of a coral wall.

When I found a silver shoe glittering
in the gutter like a fallen star.

When I birthed and birthed and birthed.
What is life but a pulley, a small

machine, animated until it's not?
Where we live, icicles are myth,

and caves form underwater. In the weeds,
we find seawater and more seawater.

Yesterday, my friend and I noticed a skirt
of ocean reaching into the park, flaring

past mangrove centurions. Tomorrow,
our city will be a spillway, a throughway,

a conduit. Isn't that all it's ever been?
Listen, my love grows inside it anyway,

a moth-bitten thing, a Phalenopsis
opening in the faintest light. O heart,

crumb-lover, taker of any bid. For as long
as there's land to walk along, isthmus,

channel, bridge to nothing, I'll move, I'll play,
I'll scrape flint into fire. As long as we have

a city to love, I'll run along its banks,
its mosaic of streets, tracing its body

like a lover's skin. I'll witness how its animals
chant to the sun, to the moon, every note

a kiss, every song a moshpit of sound.
I'll absorb its traffic, its languages, the noise

of many lives, noise of the rope, noise of the wheel,
noise of many hearts flashing, all of us lighthouses

gathering light in the darkest of times
and signing each other to safety, all the way home.

Instructions: Our Next Lifetime

When karma brings you back around,
I want you to find me, so we
can travel to southern Spain again.
You won't eat octopus. I won't eat it either,
but we'll feast on all the olives and the flesh
of blood oranges. When you come back,
I want to trace the last vestige of tomato
sauce from your plate, lapping it with crusty bread.
I'll learn the slang of my ancestors next time.
I want to tell you dirty jokes in their native
tongue. When you come back, find me
scattering red rose petals, white jasmine
flowers, and lotus buds in a temple while thinking
your name. Find me on a beach at sunrise.
Find me walking the shore, stepping around broken shells.
Find me racing down a city block. Find
my body moving in the direction of its longing.
Find me plunging into oceans, into rivers,
and lakes. Find my eyes scaling mountains.
Find me whispering to the sacred ficus
tree in my backyard, every word moving
like song up the tree's spine from canopy
to roots. Find me tying gold threads and glass bracelets
around the tree. Find me planted there.
Next time around, press your ear
to the ground. Feel my voice calling you.

Ode

I am the daughter of the daughter of the daughter of immigrants.

I am the daughter of temperate islands, of rich, rip-current oceans.

I am the daughter of fresh-dug potatoes, of hand-rolled pasta, of seasonal cherry and apple pies.

I am the daughter of lime-green spring buds, of ochre-and-rust autumn leaves.

I am the daughter of pear orchards, berry fields, of green mountains and still lakes.

I am the daughter of quiet, of silence, of cold, of wooden church pews and Sunday jelly donuts.

I am the daughter of boredom, of busy, of the step stool and the ladder.

I am the daughter of obey and because I said so.

I am the daughter of kick-the-can, of sardines and hide and seek, of roller skates and hopscotch.

I am the daughter of motorhome dreams, of travel, of the open road.

I am the daughter of disco, of Otis Redding, of Roberta Flack, of Elvis and the Beatles.

I am the daughter of libraries, of books, of tomes, of poems, of questions too big for one mind.

I am the daughter of wonder, of bewilderment, of a sacred, sacred heart.

I am the daughter of dreams (can I say that enough?), of a better life, of migration and movement.

I am the daughter of labor, of dirt-under-the-nails, of worn soles.

I am the daughter of hours-on-her-feet, of aching legs and restless hands.

I am the daughter of the daffodils' return, of forsythia branches, each star-flower constellating hope.

I am the daughter of soft-serve Coney Island ice cream, splintered boardwalks, and ocean roars.

I am the daughter of city soot and country sweet grass.

I am the daughter of I'll do what I want, thank you; I am the daughter of survival.

I am the daughter of cells divided, of genes swimming from one generation to another.

I am the daughter of four continents, many languages spoken, many gods worshiped.

I am the daughter of carbon and oxygen, of bone and body, bound by phases of the moon, bound by sky.

I am the daughter passing through with you, spinning under stars, turning with the earth.

I am the daughter with her own axis.

I am the daughter of the universe, a comet surging, walking, running, dancing across this earth.

I am the daughter of one life, of many lives, of subatomic particles, of light.

I am the daughter of the spoken and the ineffable, of one expression in time, like you and you and you and you and you.

ACKNOWLEDGEMENTS

My deep thanks to the editors and staff of the literary journals where versions of these poems first appeared:

Green Mountains Review Online: "Palm Sunday" and "Shark Valley"

Mezzo Cammin: "Accidental Garden" and "The World"

MER VOX: "Ode," "Ode," and "Black Creek Trail or Annual Bike Ride During the Pandemic When Our Usual Route Is Closed"

Nelle Journal: "6 AM"

Northwest Review: "The Tattoos I'll Never Get" and "Instructions: Our Next Lifetime"

South Florida Poetry Journal: "Ordinary Offering" and "Follow-up Visits"

Spillway: "Earth Day, 2020"

Stirring: A Literary Collection: "Reading to My Daughter About Rocks and Gemstones Before Bedtime"

SWWIM + Womanish: "Ode"

Valparaiso Poetry Review: "Aubade, South Beach"

Verse Daily: "6 AM"

West Trestle Review: "The Summer Before My Son Leaves for College"

Notes

"6 AM" is for Connor and Austen Prescott.

"Palm Sunday" is for my family.

"Aubade, South Beach" is for Austen Prescott. The seed is *el ojo de venado* (deer's eye), which wards off *mal de ojo*, the evil eye.

An underlying organizational structure of this book is the subtle body. In yoga philosophy, the subtle body contains *chakras* (cakrāṇi), in addition to other components. Chakra means, among other things, *disc* or *wheel*. These are said to be energetic centers in the subtle body which are pierced, opened, balanced, or transcended through yogic practices. Despite their immense popularity in the West, knowledge of the chakras is very esoteric, traditionally transmitted from guru to sādhaka (practitioner/devotee).

"Ode" (section I) is for the mūlādhāra cakra (root chakra).

"Birth" is for the svādhiṣṭhāna cakra (sacral chakra).

"The World" is for the anāhata cakra (heart chakra).

"Instructions: How to Heal" is for the viśuddha cakra (throat chakra).

"The Day I Lost My Fear of Death" is for the ājñā cakra (third eye chakra).

"Ode" (section V) begins at the maṇipūra cakra and ends at the ājñā cakra, reaching for sahasrāra (from the solar plexus to the third eye to the crown).

"Currency" is an ekphrastic poem that responds to "The New Ones, will free Us" by Wangechi Mutu, an installation of four bronze statues commissioned for the Metropolitan Museum of Art, NYC, and displayed in The Met's facade in 2019.

"Luck and Unluck" refers to the Taoist story of the Zen farmer. Many versions of the story exist, but the tenor is the same.

"Scar" is for my surgical oncologist, Dr. Mesko, my endocrinologist, Dr. Manzano, and the angel doctor who found my cancer, Dr. Nguyen, and for the nurses and anesthesiologists and staff at Mt. Sinai, Miami Beach. Thank you.

"Ode" (section IV) is after Wisława Szymborska's poem "Possibilities."

"Shark Valley" is for the Brito-Kron family in honor of our New Years' Day tradition. Most of the poem was dictated while biking on site.

"Earrings" is for the artist I met in Auroville, India–an intentional town, considered the concrete form of Śrī Aurobindo's vision.

"Reading to My Daughter About Rocks and Gemstones Before Bedtime" is for Celia Prescott.

"Accidental Garden" is an American sentence acrostic, a poetic form created by my brilliant friend, Jen Karetnick. The American sentence acrostic takes a 17-syllable American sentence, as defined by Allen Ginsberg, and uses it as an acrostic to build a poem.

The saint quoted in "The World" is Sri Ramana Maharshi (Tiruvannamalai, India). The "sheaths" referred to are the pañcakośas (the five sheaths) or layers (annamaya kośa, prāṇamaya kośa, manomaya kośa, vijñānamaya kośa, and ānandamaya kośa), which are peeled back or traveled through yogic practices.

"Instructions: How to Give Things Away" is indebted to E. E. Cummings.

"A Word with God" borrows a line from T.S. Eliot's "The Dry Salvages" from Four Quartets.

"Ordinary Offering" begins with a quote from my friend Dina Mitrani.

"7 PM" is for Connor Prescott.

"Black Creek Trail or Annual Bike Ride During the Pandemic When Our Usual Route Is Closed" is for my boys.

"The Summer Before My Son Leaves for College" is for Connor Prescott.

"Ode" (section V) responds to the exhibit "Childish" from Womanish in Wynwood (Miami, Florida). It is dedicated to my parents, grandparents, and great-grandparents.

GRATITUDE

This book is for my children, Connor, Austen, and Celia, three beautiful humans I have been lucky to raise. I love you.

For my family who has supported me during many years of writing, especially Andy, my husband, who's been there from the beginning and whose love and encouragement are unwavering; my grandparents, especially Helen and Lovey, the undaunted matriarchs of my family who understood little of poetry, but always encouraged my art; my parents, Joan and Vin, and my sisters, Jeanninne, Marianne, and Patty, and their families; my many cousins; my in-laws, for their compassion and acceptance; and for my extended family, especially my many aunts and uncles who have supported my work in tangible and intangible ways. Thank you to the Hanson clan, who are also family–Dan, Diane, Britta, Erika; I cannot count how many readings you've been to and how many poems (often drafts) you've read over the last two decades. Thank you for your sustained love and encouragement.

For me, writing is a solitary act polished in community. Communities of writers have kept me afloat–writing and submitting–when I didn't know if anything I wrote was worth publishing. This work wouldn't be here without them. For my friends Catherine Staples (an early, gracious reader of this manuscript) and Dean Rader (for teaching me a thing or two about titles). For my fierce and talented SWWIM sisters–Jen Karetnick, Caridad Moro-Gronlier, Alexandra Lytton Regalado, and Mary Block. Thank you for working all sides of the poetry aisle with me from organizing, to publishing, to sharing and editing our own work. For the Miami Poetas: SWWIM sisters + Emma Trelles, Mia Leonin, Elisa Albo, and Rita Maria Martinez, I love our conversations, writing prompts, and supportive collective. For the Matrix writers: Michele Kotler, Marion Wrenn, Brenda Cardenas, Janet Jennerjohn, Kristen Kaszubowski, Jane Creighton, Nicole Callihan, Robin Reagler, Laura Cronk, Suzanne Wise, Ruth Ellen Kocher, and Iris Dunkle, a handful of these poems came out of the magical Matrix; they are as much yours as they are mine. And a special shout out to Michele, who's tenacity brought me into this group of dedicated, mature, and generous writers.

For my yoga girls–Cristina and Maylen Dominguez, Britta and Erika Hanson, Carolina Garcia Jayaram, Dina and Rhonda Mitrani–my sisters in art, yoga, motherhood, and everything in between. I cherish our friendship.

For my yoga family at Ahanā Yoga (Miami, Florida), where I completed my yoga teacher training and teach yoga philosophy. Thank you, Dawn Feinberg, for creating a yoga community with spiritual roots, and for pushing me to complete your teacher training. Hari bol!

Pranams to Michael Stasko, my first philosophy teacher and dear friend, who has shared so much of his guru's (and his own) wisdom and grace with me; and to the teachers and staff at Embodied Philosophy, where I completed a 300-hour certification in Yoga Philosophy. To Edwin Bryant, whose teachings continue to refine my understanding. To Dr. Vasant Lad and Michael Stasko for their elucidation of cakrāni–from the historical to the esoteric.

To Danusha Laméris for selecting this manuscript for publication. I am elated that my work resonated with you. Thank you for receiving it with an open heart and mind. You have given me a great gift, and I am forever grateful.

To Gunpowder Press, David Starkey and Chryss Yost, for your careful eye for design and attention to the word. Thank you for your devotion to poetry and for your kindness. I am sorry I never met Barry Spacks, but I am grateful for his poetry and his legacy.

My cancer experience is my own. To the readers of this book who have received a cancer diagnosis, who are going through treatment, who are in remission, or who have lost a loved one to cancer, my heart is with you.

About the Poet

Catherine Esposito Prescott is the author of the chapbooks *Maria Sings* and *The Living Ruin*. Her work appears in many journals and anthologies, including *EcoTheo Review*, *Green Mountains Review Online*, *MER VOX*, *Mezzo Cammin*, *NELLE*, *Northwest Review*, *Pleiades*, *Spillway*, *Stirring: A Literary Collection*, *Valparaiso Poetry Review*, *Verse Daily*, and *West Trestle Review*, as well as *Grabbed: Poets & Writers on Sexual Assault, Empowerment, & Healing* and *The Orison Anthology*. Co-founder of SWWIM and Editor in Chief of *SWWIM Every Day*, Prescott earned an MFA in Creative Writing-Poetry from NYU. She leads writing and yoga retreats and teaches vinyasa yoga and yoga philosophy in Miami, where she lives with her family.

catherineespositoprescott.com

BARRY SPACKS POETRY PRIZE

2015 - Judge Dan Gerber
Instead of Sadness
Catherine Abbey Hodges

2016 - Judge Thomas Lux
Burning Down Disneyland
Kurt Olsson

2017 - Judge Jane Hirshfield
Posthumous Noon
Aaron Baker

2018 - Judge Lee Herrick
The Ghosts of Lost Animals
Michelle Bonczek Evory

2019 - Judge Stephen Dunn
Drinking with O'Hara
Glenn Freeman

2020 - Judge Jessica Jacobs
Curriculum
Meghan Dunn

2021 - Judge Lynne Thompson
Like All Light
Todd Copeland

2022 - Judge Danusha Laméris
Accidental Garden
Catherine Esposito Prescott

ALSO FROM GUNPOWDER PRESS

Mother Lode - Peg Quinn
Raft of Days - Catherine Abbey Hodges
Unfinished City - Nan Cohen
Original Face - Jim Peterson
Shaping Water - Barry Spacks
The Tarnation of Faust - David Case
Mouth & Fruit - Chryss Yost

CALIFORNIA POETS SERIES
Downtime - Gary Soto
Speech Crush - Sandra McPherson
Our Music - Dennis Schmitz
Gatherer's Alphabet - Susan Kelly-DeWitt

ALTA CALIFORNIA CHAPBOOKS
On Display - Gabriel Ibarra
Sor Juana - Florencia Milito
Levitations - Nicholas Reiner
Grief Logic - Crystal AC Salas

SHORELINE VOICES PROJECT
*Big Enough for Words: Poems and Vintage Photographs
from California's Central Coast*
David Starkey, George Yatchisin, and Chryss Yost editors
While You Wait: A Collection by Santa Barbara County Poets
Laure-Anne Bosselaar, editor
To Give Life a Shape: Poems Inspired by the Santa Barbara Museum of Art
David Starkey and Chryss Yost, editors
What Breathes Us: Santa Barbara Poets Laureate, 2005-2015
David Starkey, editor
Rare Feathers: Poems on Birds & Art
Nancy Gifford, Chryss Yost, and George Yatchisin, editors
Buzz: Poets Respond to SWARM - Nancy Gifford and Chryss Yost, editors

CPSIA information can be obtained
at www.ICGtesting.com
Printed in the USA
BVHW032008150223
658591BV00004B/276

9 781957 062068